THE TWELVE COCKTAILS

Library of Congress Cataloging-In-Publication Data Available

Authored and designed in the United States of America. Printed in China.

First Printing, July 2015

ISBN 978-09892076-1-4

Aumma, LLC
7835 South Rainbow Blvd.
Suite 4-97
Las Vegas, NV 89139

www.AummaGroup.com

This book is available in bulk at discount prices.
For more information visit www.AummaGroup.com

CONTENTS

THE TWELVE COCKTAILS

Page 4 .... Introduction

Page 5 .... About the Authors

Page 6 .... Symbols

Page 7 - 8 .... How to Use This Book

Page 9 - 12 ....Essential Bar Tools

Page 13 - 17 .... Popular Cocktail Garnishes

Page 18 - 27 .... Bartending Techniques

Page 28 - 31 .... Glassware

Page 32 ....The Twelve Cocktails Composition Chart

Page 33 ....Cocktail Ingredients

Page 34 .... Shirley Temple

Page 36 ....Gin & Tonic

Page 38 .... Black Russian

Page 40 ....Shandy

Page 42 ....Mimosa

Page 44 .... Piña Colada

Page 46 .... Manhattan

Page 48 .... Cosmopolitan

Page 50 .... Mai Tai

Page 52 ....Mojito

Page 54 ....Irish Coffee

Page 56 .... Sangria

Too often the excitement of a new gadget you just purchased is quickly over-shadowed by the six chapters you need to read in order to assemble it and the additional four you need to read to learn how to use it - not the case with this book!

This cocktail book was inspired by our desire to explain the topic of cocktails in a "let's-cut-to-the-chase" fashion. For this reason, we have spared you from information typically found at the beginning of recipe guides and we have kept only the essential and time tested information here at your fingertips.

What we *did* add to this book is our signature *Cocktail Composition Chart* (see pages 32 and 33) which gives you an overview of what is "under the hood" - the chemistry of all cocktails. This chart is worth a million words.

With *"The Twelve Cocktails"* we have utilized our combined fifty geeked-out years of experience to carefully select the twelve cocktails every Bartender or Cocktail Enthusiast needs to master.. The ingredient structure and preparation of these twelve cocktails, accompanied by our visual components, will give you the knowledge required to prepare over 1200 different cocktails!

That progression will be further covered in the sequel to this book called **"12 to 1200 Cocktails"**.

So, rather than offer another recipe book, what we offer you is a system that prepares you to execute every single relevant bartending technique you need to know to prepare any cocktail.

- Livio Lauro & Armando Rosario

"Simplicity is the ultimate sophistication."
- Leonardo da Vinci

Armando Rosario

Livio Lauro

Armando Rosario has specialized in the development of innovative cocktail creations for more than three decades. Several of his signature cocktails have appeared in trade magazines around the country such as Cheers, The Tasting Panel and Wall Street Journal. Armando has worked in such respected establishments as Le Cirque 2000 in New York, Princess Cruise Lines, and Wynn Las Vegas.

Armando graduated from Hotel Training Management School in Portugal and speaks five languages fluently; he has earned accreditations at several well recognized institutions. Armando won the prestigious award of State and National champion of the United States Bartenders' Guild (USBG) Cocktail Competition and competed in Berlin, Germany representing the USA for World Championship and achieving the highest position ever by a United States bartender In over 40 years. He has been a member of the IBA (International Bartenders Association) since 1985.

Armando lives in Orlando, Florida and presides over the 12-week Academy of Spirits and Mixology educational program Southern Wine and Spirits of Florida.

"Make it fresh...Keep it simple".

Livio Lauro started his beverage career over 20 years ago in Southern Italy on the beautiful island of Ischia in the heart of the Mediterranean.

Livio moved to the United States in 2001 and helped pioneer the resurgence of the United States Bartenders' Guild (USBG). He is the founding President of USBG Master Accreditation program; which is known as the premier national testing body for bartenders in the United States.

Since 2001, Livio has been employed by Southern Wine and Spirits in Las Vegas and works alongside the foremost distillers and beverage importers in the world. Livio has also worked with many of the most recognizable hospitality corporations by assisting them in the development of successful and profitable Beverage initiatives. He is also a frequent guest lecturer on F&B-related topics at University of Nevada, Las Vegas (UNLV); which is recognized for having the most prestigious hospitality education program in the world.

Livio is the Editor and Chief Contributor to the USBG Beverage and Bartending Compendium, which was recently included as one of the 50 cocktail books every bartender must own, spanning over 150 years.

"Every summer, for the past ten years, I have had the pleasure of getting to know Armando Rosario & Livio Lauro as we take over the kitchen and bar of Shakespeare Ranch in Lake Tahoe for Keep Memory Alive's annual rodeo.

Armando and Livio have a combined 50 years of knowledge in the beverage industry. They are a power house of knowledge in bartending and mixology, who have generously shared their expertise here. In The Twelve Cocktails™, they show readers a clever bartending system that encourages you to learn the sophisticated world of cocktails through twelve carefully selected classic drinks. Whether a cocktail enthusiast, or a bartender at any level, you will love the ease in learning how to make incredible cocktails and bar favorites.

Their approach is smart and makes cocktail creating accessible to the rest of us. I know you will enjoy this easy-to-follow collection of recipes.

- Emeril Lagasse
Chef,Restaurateur

The Meaning of our Symbols

In the next few pages you will find these symbols, please make note of their meaning. It will help you memorize the cocktail methods and come useful in quickly understanding recipes.

 BUILD Page 18 (Building Technique)

 ROLL Page 22 (Rolling Technique)

 BLEND Page 19 (Blending Technique)

 STIR Page 20 (Stirring Technique)

 SHAKE Page 21 (Shaking Technique)

 STRAIN Page 23 (Straining Technique)

 MUDDLE Page 24 (Muddling Technique)

 LAYER Page 25 (Layering Technique)

 RINSE Page 26 (Rinsing Technique)

 MARRY Page 27 (Marrying Technique)

HOW TO USE THIS BOOK

Through our presentation of *The Twelve Cocktails™*, we intend to present the reader with an easy to understand snapshot of the world of cocktails and mixed drinks. Written with the general reader in mind, this book examines and educates on cocktail topics through a visual, historical, cultural and undiluted perspective in a mere 57 pages.

We have assembled a serious and insightful summary designed to capture the interests of enthusiasts and cocktail professionals alike. Moreover, we hope to have presented this material simply enough to be accessible by anyone through our minimal use of technical terms, less prose and more visual facts.

Despite the rapid evolution in this field, we believe this book can function as a comprehensive resource for those wishing to learn about essential cocktail methods and recipes.

To assist the reader in understanding how this book is assembled, here is our vision of key learning points to be conveyed:

1. The meticulous selection of the twelve categories and the twelve cocktails
2. The importance of the history of each cocktail
3. The importance of the current culture of each cocktail
4. The importance of our symbols and our signature ***Cocktail Composition Chart***™ (page 32)

1. The thoughtful selection of the twelve categories and the twelve cocktails

Over the years, we have seen cocktails categorized in many different ways: from their base spirit, to whether they are tall or short, sweet or dry, and even how they complement a meal. Each one of these categories present some challenges on how to enhance your knowledge. For this reason, we have decided to classify cocktails based on the composition of what is in the glass and what it takes to make each cocktail well. Each cocktail was carefully selected based on popular favorites enjoyed at home or at a local bar. For instance, the *Cosmopolitan* cocktail is less historical, less crafty, and has less "character" than several of its category counterparts. However, its popularity today far surpasses any similar drink; so, in the world of cocktails that are shaken, strained and served up, the *Cosmopolitan* is the king, and that is the cocktail we will be showcasing.

2. The importance of the history of each cocktail

Why should anyone bother learning about events and ideas from long ago? Who cares anyway? We are writing this book so that you learn and remember how to make better cocktails through your knowledge of its history. In our opinion, the study of cocktail history is necessary to learn key information to help you memorize not only each cocktail's specific ingredients, but how the cocktail is made and why it was created. We believe a lack of understanding of history deprives us all of key information which can be useful when memorizing terms, executing a recipe, and talking intelligently about cocktails! After all, isn't this why you are reading this book?

3. The importance of the current culture of each cocktail

Personal customs and opinions are more significant than ever and relevant to the evolution of each classic; this of course gives each cocktail its "brand identity." While the *Gin & Tonic* was originally created for medicinal purposes, today it is a fun, refreshing, and iconic drink. Knowing this type of information ultimately allows you to "live" the essence of the cocktail, not just learn how to make it.

4. The importance of our symbols and our *Cocktail Composition Chart*™ (p.32)

Thanks to amazing advancements in technology, we are living in a very image-rich age and the dissemination of visual aids has transformed the way we learn and perceive information. Throughout this book, you will see that key topics and practices are supplemented with symbols designed to visually assist and immerse our readers in the world of each cocktail. A number of studies discovered the strength of our brain's ability to store and recall images, as opposed to text, and this cognitive ability helps shape our understanding of everything in our world from early childhood. So, for students who are being exposed to new subject areas, we believe this is the best way to facilitate effective learning of this cocktail collection.

In conclusion, we recommend you become not only familiar with the history and culture of each drink, but also take the time to understand the meaning and methodology of each cocktail, then cross reference the concepts with the cocktail symbols and graphic aids. Doing so will maximize your learning experience and allow you to understand, not just memorize, the information provided. As the saying goes: "Give a man a fish and you feed him for a day; teach a man to fish and you feed him for a lifetime." We invite you to immerse yourself and enjoy *The Twelve Cocktails*™!

Bar Spoon:
A long and often spiral-handled spoon with many different uses, including mixing, muddling, layering cocktails and extracting solid ingredients out of jars. The use of the bar spoon is key when building or stirring a cocktail because the spoon mixes and simultaneously chills the drink.

Blender:
A kitchen appliance used to mix food and other substances. Primarily used in bars is to make frozen drinks.

It is always wise to invest in a high quality blender. After all, frozen drinks are easy to consume! Once you start blending, expect it to be spinning non-stop.

Boston Shaker:
Professional bartenders prefer this shaker which consists of a tin cup and a 16-ounce mixing glass.

The benefits of this type of shaker, compared to the more traditional three piece shaker, are many. You will learn more about this on page 21.

We recommend pouring the ingredients in the mixing glass and the ice in the tin. Then, place the mixing glass over the tin and shake vigorously.

Bottle Opener:
A tool that removes metal caps from bottles. Most bartenders prefer the "speed opener" as shown here.

Citrus Peeler:
This citrus peeler is made of a hooked edge that perforates perfectly as it cuts across your fruit. It's tapered end navigates its way under the rind, allowing you to slide off the peel with the greatest of ease. This tool is seen in use on page 14.

Cork Screw:
The standard industry tool for opening a bottle of wine. It is also known as a sommelier knife, waiter's friend or wine key. Most corkscrews also have an ancillary built-in bottle cap opener.

Cutting Board:
Cutting boards are generally made of wood or plastic. Plastic boards are easier to sanitize and are preferred for cutting items like fresh fruit that can spoil. It is recommended to maintain different sizes of cutting boards.

Fruit Press (Citrus Squeezer):
A hand tool used to squeeze the fresh juice from lemons, limes or oranges designed to block a portion of the pulp from entering the cocktail. This tool is seen in use on page 24.

Hawthorne Strainer:

A round screen with a handle and spring surrounding its edge that can be placed over a mixing glass or shaker tin to hold back ice when transferring the contents from that container into a glass. (A process known as *straining*). See page 23 for usage example.

Julep Strainer:

The Julep Strainer is a perforated metal strainer in the shape of a spoon. Unlike the Hawthorne Strainers, which fit snug across the top of a Boston Shaker's tin cup, the Julep Strainer is too small for that opening. It does, however, fit gently within the Mixing Glass at an angle. See page 23 for usage example.

Jigger:

Measuring cocktail ingredients is key. The jigger is a small, conical metal or plastic measuring device that comes in various sizes with one end of the cup containing a larger amount than the other end. Sizes can range from ½ ounce to 2 ounces depending on what is purchased.

Knife:

A cutting tool necessary to slice fruit, but also useful in carving special garnishes. Similar to the cutting board, it is recommended to maintain different knife sizes so you are prepared to work on any fruit regardless of its size. Maintaining sharp knives is key to easy cutting and beautiful garnishes.

Ice Scoop:

Typically made of metal or heavy plastic, the ice scoop is key for handling ice in a quick and measured way. For sanitation reasons, it should always have a handle.

Ice scoops can be purchased in different sizes, and we recommend a 12 oz. scoop as it is the most common size for making one drink.

Muddler:

A pestle, usually made of hardwood, metal, or food-safe plastic, typically used to mash or muddle the hard chunks of sugar, herbs, fruits, etc., in the bottom of a glass or shaker to release flavor. Larger muddlers make muddling much easier and are preferred by professional bartenders. See page 24 for usage example.

Pour Spout:

A reusable spouted device that is placed in the neck of bottles to regulate the flow of the liquid. Pour spouts are available in a variety of shapes and styles. Pour spouts come in different portion sizes depending on how fast a liquid flows through them. A benefit to using them is the ability to mentally count while pouring and control each and every portion.

Vegetable Peeler:

This vegetable peeler is a must-have for quick garnishing. It is sharp stainless steel blade is great for peeling oranges, lemons, limes and more.

(See page 14 for a quick way to make a lemon peel, under "lemon twists with a shortcut").

Garnishes are very important to cocktails; they enhance the appearance and often add positive subtleties to the flavor. Preparing your garnishes really depends on what drinks you are going to be serving. Not all of the below are necessary unless you plan on having a full bar where anything might be requested. In that case, these would be your essentials:

Cherries: Maraschino Cherries are used for many cocktails, including the *Shirley Temple, Mai Tai, Manhattan* and *Piña Colada*. You can buy them at the grocery store. They come in a jar ready to use.

Olives: There are many different olives on the market today. Some olives come plain and some come stuffed with peppers or other ingredients. They come in a jar ready to use. For a standard bar setup we recommend Pimento Olives.

Cocktail Onions: Cocktail Onions are pearl onions pickled in brine. They have a crispy and subtle sweet flavor that can compliment all kinds of dry cocktails. You can buy them at the grocery store. They come in a jar ready to use.

Kosher Salt: Kosher Salt is used to coat the rim of a glass. Moisten the rim of a glass with a citrus fruit followed by a dip into this salt.

Lemon Wedges: Cut off the tips of a lemon. Then cut the lemon in half lengthwise from one end to the other. Cut each half into four equal wedges. One lemon should yield eight wedges.

1.

2.

3.

4.

Lemon Twists: Cut one half inch off each sides of a lemon, then, with the use of a Citrus Peeler, cut the white pith to separate the skin from the flesh. Remove the flesh from the peel. Roll up the peel and slice into 1/4" pieces. Roughly four to six twists should result.

1.

2.

3.

4.

Lemon Twists (Peels) with a Short Cut: Use the Vegetable Peeler as shown below.

14

Lime Wheels: Cut off one end of a lime. Then cut slices crosswise from one end to the other. Use your judgment on how thick the slices should be. Finally, make one cut from the center of the lime wheel to the edge so it can sit on the glass.

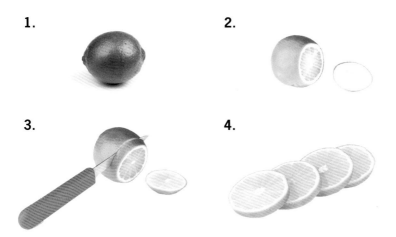

1.   **2.**

3.   **4.**

Lime Wedges: Cut off both tips of a lime. Then, cut the lime in half lengthwise from one end to the other. Depending on the size, cut each half into two or four equal wedges.

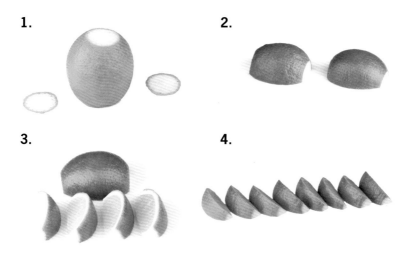

1.   **2.**

3.   **4.**

Orange Slices: Cut off one end of the orange. Next, cut the fruit in half from one end to the other. Finally cut both halves into slices.

1. **2.**

3. **4.**

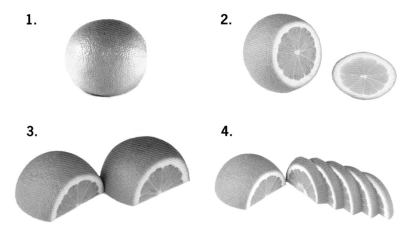

Pineapple Wedges: Cut off the top of the pineapple. Then cut only a few slices cross wise from one end to another. Use your judgement on how thick the slices should be. Finally, cut wedges as shown below.

1. **2.**

3. **4.**

Mint Leaves: Wash the mint leaves with water only. Pluck the leaves and place them in a container with water, as well. Set aside the mint tops in a separate container with water.

Whipped Cream: You can buy a can of whipped cream at the store or you can whip it yourself. Whichever you choose, we are not here to judge you!

or

Simple Syrup: Combine equal parts of hot water (between 170° and 185° degrees Fahrenheit) and granulated sugar. Store your syrup in a sterile glass container and keep refrigerated.

Building: When "building" a cocktail, the ingredients are poured into the glass in which the cocktail will be served. A bar spoon or swizzle stick is used to stir the ingredients before serving (a practice far too often omitted.)

1. Fill serving glass with ice

2. Pour in alcohol base

4. Stir ingredients

3. Pour in secondary ingredient(s)

5. Garnish & serve

18

Blending: An electric blender is needed for recipes containing fruit or other ingredients which do not break down from "shaking". "Blending" is an appropriate method of combining these ingredients with others, creating a smooth ready-to-serve drink.

1. Pour in alcohol base

4. Blend ingredients until texture is smooth

2. Pour in secondary ingredient(s)

3. Add ice

5. Pour drink, garnish & serve

Stirring: You can "stir" cocktails effectively with a bar spoon in a mixing glass. If ice is to be used, use ice cubes to prevent dilution and strain the contents into a glass when the surface of the mixing glass begins to collect condensation.

1. Collect your mixing glass, Julep Strainer and Bar Spoon

2. Add Ice to mixing glass

4. Stir ingredients until cold

3. Pour in all ingredients

5. Strain and garnish cocktail

Shaking: When a drink contains fruit juices, syrups, cream, or even eggs, it is necessary to "shake" the ingredients. This method requires the use of a cocktail shaker (see Boston Shaker on p.9) to mix ingredients together and chill them simultaneously. Normally, this is done with ice cubes filling the mixing glass three-quarters of the way full. When you have poured in the ingredients, hold the shaker and give a short, sharp, snappy shake. When water has begun to condense on the surface of the shaker, the cocktail should be sufficiently chilled and ready to be strained (as shown on p.23) or poured directly in the glass.

1. Pour ingredients in mixing glass and add ice to the mixing tin

4. Tap the side with palm of your hand to release seal and open

2. Seal and tap

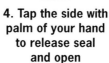

3. Shake for 10 seconds

5. Your cocktail is ready to be strained or poured

Rolling: "Rolling" is a good technique used to mix and chill cocktails that have ingredients which do not take well to a hard shake such as sparkling beverages, milk and other ingredients that tend to froth when shaken. To roll your drink you'll need two glasses or one glass and a cocktail shaker. Fill one glass to the top with ice then add your cocktail ingredients. Pour the contents from this glass into another glass or cocktail shaker. Return your cocktail ingredients to the original glass going back and fourth a few times. Then strain (as shown on p.23) or pour the drink directly into the glass.

**Roll drink from
right to left**

**Roll drink back
from left to right**

Straining: When a drink calls for straining, place the appropriate strainer (Hawthorne or Julep) on top of your shaker tin or mixing glass and pour.

**Straining
with Julep Strainer**

**Straining into
cocktail glass**

**Double straining
solid ingredients**

Muddling: To extract the most flavor from certain fresh ingredients, such as fruit and herbs, you should crush the ingredient with the pestle, using the back end of most bar spoons, or with a muddler.

1. Add solid ingredient(s)

2. Add 1 liquid ingredient, preferably non-alcoholic

4. Add ice and remaining liquid ingredient(s)

3. Muddle ingredients together

5. Garnish and serve

Layering: To layer or float an ingredient on top of another. In cocktail preparation, the floating substance can be either liquid (such as Liqueurs) or semisolid (such as Whipped Cream). Learning the approximate weight and density of certain liqueurs will allow you to complete this technique more successfully. There are several on-line tools that provide this information by ingredient.

In the case of floating one liquid on top of another, the goal is to pour the different liquids so gently that the surface tension of the previous ingredient remains intact; this will prevent any mixing. So you need a steady hand and the use of the rounded or back part of a spoon. Slowly pour down the spoon and into the glass (as seen on the picture below on the left). The ingredient should run down the inside of the glass and remain separated from the ingredient below it.

In the case of adding a dollop of a semisolid ingredient on top of a liquid, the use of a large spoon to ladle the ingredient into the glass (as seen on the picture below on the right) is much easier.

Option 1: Pour the floating ingredient over a spoon to buffer the force of the ingredient and let it gently pour into the cocktail

Option 2: Pour the floating ingredient from the spoon into the cocktail

Rinse: A "Rinse" (AKA "Wash") is the method of coating the inside of a glass with a liquid (mostly bold alcoholic ingredients), then discarding the excess liquid, before pouring the drink into it. It provides a hint of flavor which compliments the cocktail when done properly. Pour ¼ ounce of your rinse ingredient into the glass. Swirl and tip the glass so the liquid coats the sides and the rim of the glass. Discard excess rinse.

1. Pick serving glass

2. Pour 1/4 ounce into glass

3. Swirl Glass 360°

4. Drain excess liquid

5. Glass is ready for cockatil

26

In the creation of cocktails, there are a few cases where ingredients need time to be either softened, enhanced or both. These techniques require experience and patience to learn, so take your time! In most cocktail books, these techniques are not grouped into the same chapter as we have done here, but since they all require "marrying" time to prepare, we feel there are enough similarities to keep them together.

1. Pre-batching Cocktails: This process simply consists of building many cocktails of a single variation by multiplying a single recipe times the desired amount of servings. The benefits to pre-batching are to serve consistent tasting and quickly served drinks at special gatherings by pre-pouring all the ingredient into a pitcher. Keep the pitcher refrigerated and pour the pre-batch for guests a' la minute. Always add any sparkling ingredients at service time.

2. Pre-batching Steeped Cocktails: This practice is similar to the process above, but in addition to the liquid ingredients, it incorporates the steeping of a variety of solid ingredients. These solid ingredients, such as fruits or herbs, are added in the same manner as in the preparation of Sangria (see page 56).

Tip for steeping: Slice your solid ingredients finely to increase their surface area and speed up the flavoring time, remove any pits, seeds, or stems and keep refrigerated. Daily tasting (and logging) of your concoction along with your personal preferences will be of utmost importance in determining your final recipes.

3. Barrel-Aging Cocktails: This process consists of pouring all-alcoholic cocktail ingredients (such as the ingredients in a Manhattan) into small barrels and allowing them to interact with the wood for a few weeks or months. Aged cocktails deliver the added vanilla and caramel sweetness that come with the time in the oak aging. We recommend starting with a small 1 gallon barrel and seasoning it with an inexpensive fortified wine for a week or so, and draining it when it's time to make the cocktail. Once you have chosen which cocktail you wish to age, meticulously measure and log your portions so you can replicate and adjust future recipes.

There are a few more "marrying" instances which are typically reserved for single ingredients such as alcoholic infusions, flavored syrups, tinctures, and bitters. These practices do not create cocktails – just individual cocktail ingredients that can replace store-bought products.

ROCKS GLASS

Rocks Glass:
The Rocks Glass is a short tumbler used for serving an alcoholic beverage, such as whiskey over ice ("on the rocks"). It is also normally used to serve certain cocktails, such as the *Old-Fashioned*, which became synonymous with the "Rocks Glass". Today "Old-Fashioned" glass means Rocks Glass. The traditional size varies from 8 to 12 oz.

COLLINS GLASS

Collins Glass:
The same shape as a highball glass, the Collins Glass is bigger, holding from 10 to 14 oz. Once used solely for the mixing of the *Tom Collins* cocktail, the glass became practical for a variety of drinks, thus making it a bar essential.

TEMPERED MUG

Tempered Mug:
Tempered glass was developed in the early 1900s to withstand high temperatures. This type of glass has been pre-stressed by heating, followed by sudden quenching to give it two to four times the strength of ordinary glass. This type of mug is widely used for hot drinks such as the *Irish Coffee*. Size can range from 6 oz to 14 oz. Be sure to look under the glass to verify that the glass is heat resistent.

SHOT GLASS

Shot Glass:
A shot glass is a small glass designed to hold or measure spirits, usually between 1 oz. and 2 oz., which is either drunk straight from the glass ("a shot") or poured into a cocktail. A shot glass is sometimes known as a jigger. These glasses are available in basic shapes and sizes and can also be decorative or unique in nature. While glass is the most common form, they can also be made of plastic or metal.

COCKTAIL GLASS

Cocktail Glass:
The cocktail glass is often referred to as a Martini glass; The purpose of the cocktail glass is to serve a shaken or stirred drink, without ice. The stem lifts the bowl of the glass up and away from your hands, which would otherwise warm the cocktail. Contemporary Cocktail glasses come in many sizes (the original size was 4.5 ounces), styles, materials and colors but their purpose still remains the same.

BRANDY SNIFTER

Brandy Snifter:
Brandy Snifter (also called Cognac glass, or Balloon) is a type of glass with a short-stem whose bowl has a wide bottom and a relatively narrow top. It is mostly used to serve aged brown spirits. The rounded bottom allows the glass to be cupped in the hand, thus warming the spirit. Most snifters will hold between 8 to 20 oz., but are almost always only filled to a small part of their capacity.

BEER GLASS

Beer Glass / Mug:
Beer Glass / Mugs are as diverse as beer itself. Certain beers have a specific glass style associated with them. These styles compliment the beer for a variety of reasons, including enhancing aroma, appearance, and/or having an effect on the beer head. The most common beer glass is the Pilsner glass (as seen here) or the pint glass. Most common sizes are 12 or 16 ounces.

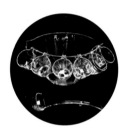

PUNCH BOWL WITH LADLE

Punch Bowl with Ladle:
A demispherical bowl that allows large mixes or punches to be prepared ahead of time. In addition to making a beautiful center piece it allows guests to serve themselves adding a communal element to the beverage.

PITCHER

Pitcher:
Pitchers are great vessels designed for entertaining on special occasions or for simple, everyday use. They are made of many different materials, such as glass, ceramic, terra-cotta and stainless steel. Pitchers are traditionally used for Sangrias and are ideal for serving large groups and pre-batched cocktails.

RED WINE GLASS

Red Wine Glasses:
Red wine glasses are tall and wide to allow the complexities of the wine to be better appreciated. Sizes vary greatly (20 oz. and up) and are usually large, but only a small part of their capacity is filled, leaving plenty of room to accentuate the best attributes of the wine.

WHITE WINE GLASS

White Wine Glasses:
White wine glasses vary in size and shape and have a smaller mouth than red wine glasses which helps keep the wine cool and reduce the rate of oxidation. The capacity of a white wine glass is approximately 13 oz..

CHAMPAGNE FLUTE

Champagne Flute:
The Champagne flute is tall and thin. Reducing the surface area at the opening of the bowl allows the bubbles to build up properly and keeps the carbonation from dissipating. The flute has largely replaced the champagne coupe or saucer, the shape of which allowed carbonation to dissipate even more rapidly. Typical Size is 7.5 oz to 10 oz..

THE TWELVE COCKTAILS COMPOSITION CHART™

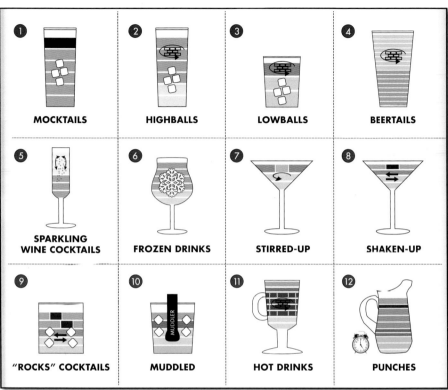

1. MOCKTAILS
2. HIGHBALLS
3. LOWBALLS
4. BEERTAILS
5. SPARKLING WINE COCKTAILS
6. FROZEN DRINKS
7. STIRRED-UP
8. SHAKEN-UP
9. "ROCKS" COCKTAILS
10. MUDDLED
11. HOT DRINKS
12. PUNCHES

TECHNIQUES

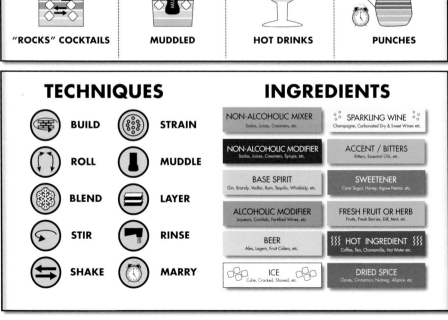

BUILD   STRAIN

ROLL   MUDDLE

BLEND   LAYER

STIR   RINSE

SHAKE   MARRY

INGREDIENTS

NON-ALCOHOLIC MIXER
Sodas, Juices, Creamers, etc.

SPARKLING WINE
Champagne, Carbonated Dry & Sweet Wines etc.

NON-ALCOHOLIC MODIFIER
Sodas, Juices, Creamers, Syrups, etc.

ACCENT / BITTERS
Bitters, Essential Oils, etc.

BASE SPIRIT
Gin, Brandy, Vodka, Rum, Tequila, Whisk(e)y, etc.

SWEETENER
Cane Sugar, Honey, Agave Nectar, etc.

ALCOHOLIC MODIFIER
Liqueurs, Cordials, Fortified Wines, etc.

FRESH FRUIT OR HERB
Fruits, Fresh Berries, Dill, Mint, etc.

BEER
Ales, Lagers, Fruit Ciders, etc.

HOT INGREDIENT
Coffee, Tea, Chamomille, Hot Water etc.

ICE
Cube, Cracked, Shaved, etc.

DRIED SPICE
Cloves, Cinnamon, Nutmeg, Allspice, etc.

32

COCKTAIL INGREDIENTS

Sweeteners:
Cane Sugar, Honey, Agave Nectar, Maple Syrup, Simple Syrup etc.

Non-Alcoholic Mixers & Second Non-Alcoholic Mixer:
Sodas, Juices, Water, Creams etc.

Sparkling Wines:
Champagne, Carbonated Dry & Sweet Wines etc.

Alcoholic Modifiers: Flavored Alcohol
Liqueurs, Cordials, Fortified Wines, Dessert Wines etc.

Ice
Cube, Cracked, Shaved, Block

Base Spirits: Distilled Alcohol
Gin, Vodka, Rum, Tequila, Whisk(e)y, Brandy, Eau-de-vie etc.

Beers / Ciders:
Ales, Lagers, Fruit Ciders, etc.

Accents / Bitters:
Bitters, Flavored Syrups, Essential Oils, Concentrates etc.

Fresh Fruit / Herbs:
Fruits, Fresh Berries, Basil, Mint, Rosemary, Dill, etc.

Hot Ingredients:
Coffee, Tea, Chamomille, Hot Water etc.

Dried Spices:
Cloves, Cinnamon, Peppercorn, Nutmeg, Allspice, etc.

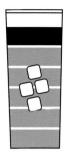

SHIRLEY TEMPLE

Ingredients:

● 5 oz. Ginger Ale or Lemon Lime Soda
● 1 oz. Grenadine Syrup

Glassware: Collins glass

Method: Build this drink directly in the glass by pouring the Ginger Ale and the Grenadine over ice and mixing with a Bar Spoon.

Garnish: Cocktail Cherry

MOCKTAILS CHEMISTRY

Also known as Non-Alcoholic Cocktails, these refreshing concoctions are a delicious must for every occasion. Made with the complete absence of alcohol, these drinks are an excellent option for designated drivers, pregnant women, kids, or anybody who does not want to drink alcohol. At their basic level, this category of drink is comprised of a key non-alcoholic ingredient (such as lemonade, a juice or a soda) which has then been further flavored with the addition of one or more non-alcoholic ingredients. The proportions used to mix these drinks can vary based on the ingredients used. For instance, in the case of the "Arnold Palmer", you use roughly 50% Iced Tea and 50% of Lemonade because both ingredients have similar dominance in flavor, however in the case of our chosen drink, the "Shirley Temple", you use roughly 85% of Ginger Ale and only 15% of Grenadine syrup because of the thick and sweet nature of the Grenadine. The Shirley Temple is the key drink from this category.

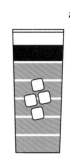

2ND
NON-ALCOHOLIC MIXER

NON-ALCOHOLIC MIXER

ICE

CHEMISTRY

SHIRLEY TEMPLE CULTURE

The Shirley Temple: every child's favorite adult-esque mocktail! Like the legendary child actress from which it is named, this drink is sweet, innocent and irresistible.

Often ordered by children who are dining out with adults, the Shirley Temple brings back memories of family gatherings and represents perhaps the humble beginnings of a future cocktail lover. Simply pour Ginger Ale or lemon-lime soda over cubes of ice and add a splash of grenadine. Its festive red color and maraschino cherry garnish offer a sophisticated alternative to the average soft drink. Serve it up with a squiggly straw, and you can be sure the kids won't be able to resist the allure of this mocktail.

The Shirley Temple is also an excellent non-alcoholic alternative to offer designated drivers.

SHIRLEY TEMPLE HISTORY

There are at least three stories from the late 1930's on the origin of this sparkling red drink. One is that it was created at Hollywood's Chasen's Restaurant to celebrate the star Shirley Temple's 10th birthday. Another claim comes from the Royal Hawaiian Hotel in Waikiki.

Finally, the Brown Derby Restaurant in Hollywood, another popular hangout for the young star is also often cited as the inventor.

Since Sardi's Restaurant in New York offered an earlier version of it called the "Kiddie cocktail", we believe that the drink had been around for some time before somebody decided to put her name on it. Oddly enough, she claimed she actually never liked the drink.

GIN & TONIC

Ingredients:

- 2 oz. Gin
- 4 oz. Tonic Water

Glassware: Highball glass

Method: Build this drink directly in the glass by pouring the gin and the tonic over ice and mix with a Bar Spoon.

Garnish: Lime slice or wedge

HIGHBALLS

Highballs are the most commonly consumed category of alcoholic mixed beverages at bars. These beverages are easy to make, easy to drink and are very food-friendly thanks to their ability to quench thirst and flush food. They also only require a very basic mixing knowledge and the only tools needed to make them is an ice scoop and a bar spoon.

At their basic level, this category of drink is "built" directly in the serving glass and consists of a base spirit which has then been enhanced and softened with a generous portion of one or more non-alcoholic ingredients giving them their characteristically easy-drinking quality. Examples from this category are the Cuba Libre (Rum, Cola and Lime Juice) or the Cape Cod (Vodka and Cranberry Juice), however the king of this category is the "Gin & Tonic" which is typically comprised of 30% Gin and 70% Tonic Water (Quinine).

NON-ALCOHOLIC MIXER
Sodas, Juices, Creamers, etc.

BASE SPIRIT
Gin, Brandy, Vodka, Rum, Tequila, Whisk(e)y, etc.

ICE
Cube, Cracked, Shaved, etc.

The Gin & Tonic (AKA G&T) is a piney, fizzy offering of simple sophistication. Marvel at the stack of cubed ice in the glass and hear the gentle hiss of bubbles; this is what the G&T is all about! We are aware of at least three different dates celebrated as International Gin and Tonic Day, which is a testament to the iconic status of the G&T.

While acknowledging the importance of good ice and fresh citrus garnish, the two main players here are premium Gin and quality Tonic Water. This stunning combination creates a somewhat medicinal taste, but delivers a crisp refreshing flavor that can only be described as the envy of any highball.

James Bond prefers his G&T with the juice of an entire lemon, but many will appreciate how it pairs effortlessly with salty, fatty morsels, thus making it a food-friendly drink.

The Gin & Tonic came about for medicinal reasons; it was originally developed in the mid 1800's by British Officers to help fight malaria. The officers were stationed in India where they became susceptible to the disease.

They found out that quinine, an ingredient found in tonic water, helped get rid of the disease even though it had a bitter and unpleasant taste. Eventually they mixed the Peruvian quinine extract with soda water, sugar, and gin. Instead of drinking the medicine with their troops at dawn, the officers enjoyed it at cocktail hour.

The predecessor to today's Gin & Tonic was born, and it soon became the quintessential drink of the British Empire.

BLACK RUSSIAN

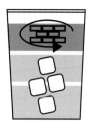

Ingredients:
- 2 oz. Vodka
- 1 oz. Coffee Liqueur

Glassware: Old Fashioned

Method: Build this drink directly in the glass by pouring the Vodka and the coffee liqueur over ice and mix with a Bar Spoon.

Garnish: None

"BUILT" LOWBALLS

This category of drink is most commonly consumed in the evening. These bold concoctions are easier for the novice drinker to make than they are to consume. At their basic level, this category of drink is "built" directly in the serving glass and is comprised of a base spirit which has been "taken to the next level" through the addition of a small portion of one or more alcoholic ingredients. This gives it a "masculine" quality and high alcohol content.

While several famous drinks such as the Godfather (Scotch & Amaretto) or the "Rusty Nail" (Scotch & Drambuie) are members of this category, the most commonly ordered drink from this catagory is the "Black Russian"; typically comprised of nearly 65% Vodka (roughly 2 fluid ounces when served in a 8 ounce "Rocks glass" with ice) and 35% premium Coffee Liqueur (1 fluid ounce when served in 8 ounce "Rocks glass" with ice).

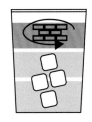

ALCOHOLIC MODIFIER
Liqueurs, Cordials, Fortified Wines, etc.

BASE SPIRIT
Gin, Brandy, Vodka, Rum, Tequila, Whisk(e)y, etc.

ICE
Cube, Cracked, Shaved, etc.

CHEMISTRY

BLACK RUSSIAN CULTURE

Dark, Mysterious, Delicious, and simple…The Black Russian is a great after-dinner cocktail and popular nightcap, offering a touch of sophistication to any occasion. The Black Russian tastes a bit like a mix of coffee and chocolate. It leads with a syrupy sweetness followed by a hint of roasted bitter char, showcasing its bold flavors and unique straightforwardness. Easy to make, this cocktail is a popular favorite the world over and is often one of the first drinks that a bartender learns to prepare.

As with many classic cocktails, the Black Russian has been modified and has evolved with the combination of other ingredients to create entirely different cocktails. The Black Russian is the favorite of a certain English gentleman. To whom do we refer? Bond… James Bond, of course!

BLACK RUSSIAN HISTORY

The "Black Russian" was created in 1949 at the Hotel Metropole in Brussels by Belgian Bartender Gustave Tops. Gustave prepared it for Perle Mesta, the ambassador of The United States in Luxemborg who was visiting his bar. It was here that the Black Russian was born.

The Cold War was just starting and the name "Black Russian" allegedly was in reference to the Soviet Union's tense relations with Europe and the United States.

In the early 1960's, the White Russian, a variation of the Black Russian, started to make its appearance in print and gain popularity. Its recipe added cream or milk to the Black Russian and its quick rise in popularity was most likely a result of its creamy and easy-drinking nature.

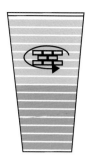

SHANDY

Ingredients:

8 oz. Lager Beer

8 oz. Lemon-lime soda

Glassware: Beer Glass

Method: Prepare this drink directly in a chilled pint glass by gently pouring the Beer and the lemon-lime soda; stir gently with a bar spoon

Garnish: None

"BEERTAILS"

Beertails are mixed drinks that continue to grow in popularity. Beer cocktails require a more gentle handling than traditional mixed drinks due to the "temperamental" nature of their easy-foaming elements (Beer or Cider). Today, Bartenders and Mixologists continue to find different ingredients (alcoholic and non) to mix with Beer and Cider. This category of drink is characterized by the fact that one of these two ingredients are incorporated in the drink.

At their basic level, this category of drink is comprised of a generous portion of Beer and/or Cider which has been flavored or modified by one or more alcoholic or non-alcoholic ingredients. Popular members of this family are drinks like the Michelada and the Red Beer. The best example comes from the "Shandy"; comprised of 50% of lemon lime soda (Roughly 8 fluid ounces when served in a 16 ounce Pint glass with no ice) and 50% of Lager beer.

BEER
Ales, Lagers, Fruit Ciders, etc.

NON-ALCOHOLIC MIXER
Sodas, Juices, Creamers, etc.

CHEMISTRY

What do you get when you elevate America's favorite brewed beverage with the addition of other delicious ingredients? An undeniably quaffable, warm-weather treat known as the Shandy! This Shandy might be the best way to quench thirst on a hot day. Although widely consumed in Britain, the Shandy is also very popular in Germany and Austria, where it is known as a Radler. In France and Italy, it's known as Panache.

This pub-favorite is lightly alcoholic, yet refreshing and is ideal for backyard BBQ's, poolside parties or anywhere you need a little hydration to complement your culinary offerings. While the original Shandy recipe was a mixture of beer and lemonade, the term now represents a category of drinks consisting of beer mixed with citrus-flavored soda, carbonated lemonade, ginger beer, and ginger ale or cider.

The Shandy is believed to have originated in Germany in the early 1900's, its name derives from the German word "schande" (shame). There are a few stories on its creation.

One states that it was developed for people to have a drink in hot weather in regions where water was unsafe to drink. Another story ties-in the drink's original name, "radler" (cyclist):

A group of German cyclists stopped by a pub for a refreshing drink. The pub got busy and the bartender realized that he may run out of beer so he started serving it mixed with a carbonated lemonade or soda to make it last longer. The cyclists loved its refreshing taste and started asking for it along their travels.

SHANDY HISTORY

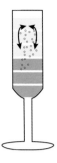

MIMOSA

Ingredients:

 2 oz. Orange Juice

4 oz. Dry Sparkling Wine

Glassware: Champagne flute

Method: We recommend preparing this drink in a mixing glass with just a few ice cubes and rolling the contents back and forth as seen on read page22. Strain the cocktail into the flute.

Garnish: None

SPARKLING WINE COCKTAILS

Often known as Champagne cocktails, these sparkling concoctions are typically prepared with previously-chilled ingredients without ice; or occasionally in a mixing glass (or tin cup) where a minimal amount of ice is used. The delicate nature of sparkling wine and the typical tiny bubbles found in high quality sparkling wine require very gentle mixing and minimal dilution from water.

At their basic level, this category of drink is served in a flute (or cocktail glass) and is comprised of a Sparkling wine which has then been flavored or modified by one or more alcoholic or non-alcoholic ingredients giving them an additional unique element.

A prime example of this is seen in a "Mimosa"; comprised of 40% orange juice (Roughly 2 fluid ounces when served in 8 ounce Champagne flute with no ice) and 60% high quality dry sparkling wine juice (Roughly 4 fluid ounces when served in an 8 ounce Champagne flute with no ice).

SPARKLING WINE
Champagne, Carbonated Dry & Sweet Wines etc.

NON-ALCOHOLIC MIXER
Sodas, Juices, Creamers, etc.

CHEMISTRY

MIMOSA CULTURE

Have you ever heard of a "Champagne Breakfast"? Ideally, such an occasion would include the Mimosa as a beverage. Mimosas are simple, refreshing and low in alcohol.

This classic brunch drink made with chilled orange juice and dry Sparkling Wine is often consumed with friends and is a popular Apéritif beverage thanks to the combination of the lovely effervescence and natural sweetness of its ingredients. As in the case of a Bloody Mary, the Mimosa cleverly covers-up its alcohol pretending to be a fruit drink.

The name "Mimosa" comes from a bright orange or yellow tropical flower called acacia dealbata, and this drink is arguably the most food-accompanied cocktail in existence. Its low alcoholic content makes it an acceptable option when other cocktails may be too heavy.

MIMOSA HISTORY

This effervescent cocktail is called a Mimosa in America and a Buck's Fizz in England.

There are two stories about the origin of this orange juice and dry sparkling wine "marriage." One states that it was invented at the Ritz Hotel in Paris in 1925 by Barman Frank Meier, where it was named after the orange flower interestingly enough in his 1933 cocktail book he cites the Mimosa but does not take credit for creating it.

The other story states that the Buck's Fizz, a similar drink using a slightly different ratio of dry sparkling wine and orange juice predates the Mimosa originated in England at London's Buck's Club where it was created by one of the Barmen, Pat McGarry in 1921.

PIÑA COLADA

Ingredients:

○ 2 oz. Light Rum
○ 4 oz. Piña Colada Mix*

Glassware: Hurricane Glass

Method: Prepare this drink directly in the blender by pouring the Rum and the Colada mix over a scoop of ice and blend until smooth

Garnish: Cocktail Cherry (Optional Pineapple Spear)

*Piña Colada Mix: You can use store bought (Again, we are not here to judge you) or you can make it at home (Blend 2 Cups pineapple juice, 1 Cup coconut cream, ½ Cup half & half).

FROZEN DRINKS

These slushy concoctions are easy to make once you are stocked with plenty of ice and a hard-working blender! At their basic level this category of drink is "built and blended" in a blender cup and is comprised of a base spirit (such as Gin, or Vodka, or Rum, or Tequila, or Whiskey, or Brandy) which is then blended with a generous portion of one or more non-alcoholic ingredients and a rich portion of ice, giving them their creamy texture and no-alcohol taste.

A prime example of this is seen in a "Piña Colada"; typically comprised of 40% (Roughly 4 fluid ounces when served in a 16 ounce Hurricane glass) of Piña Colada Mix (Either store bought or home-made as listed on the bottom of page 44) 40% of slushed (blended) ice and 20% (2 fluid ounces) of light or gold rum.

NON-ALCOHOLIC MIXER
Sodas, Juices, Creamers, etc.

BASE SPIRIT
Gin, Brandy, Vodka, Rum, Tequila, Whisk(e)y, etc.

Plug-in your blenders and turn on the celebratory music! Frozen drinks will bring to life any festive or warm-weather gathering. The Piña Colada gained global popularity and solidified its place in popular lexicon after being featured in Rupert Holmes' number one song entitled "Escape."

The Piña Colada is the most popular frozen cocktail in the world! Its name comes from the Spanish words for "strained pineapple" ("Piña" = Pineapple + "Colada" = Strained).

This classic drink is the perfect complement to a hot day at the beach or the pool deck. Sip it and you will immediately begin to decompress and reinvigorate! Often overly creamy, watery, or too sweet due to poor ingredients commonly used in high volume bars, when made with fresh ingredients, the Piña Colada is undeniably delicious!

A cocktail named Piña Colada was first mentioned in 1922 in a Travel magazine article. However, the Piña Colada as we know it today was created in 1954. The Bartender widely recognized as the creator is Mr. Ramon Marrero "Monchito" who experimented with the recipe for a while.

Allegedly, Marrero created the drink at the Caribe Hilton's Beachcomber Bar in San Juan, Puerto Rico to capture all the flavors of his country in a glass.

Mr. Marrero received numerous awards and recognition for his creation. Notably, in 1978, the government declared the Piña Colada to be the official drink of Puerto Rico. Monchito served his famous drink to thousands of hotel guests and celebrities.

MANHATTAN

Ingredients:

- 2 ¼ oz. Bourbon or Rye Whiskey
- ¾ oz. Sweet Vermouth
- Dash of Angostura Bitters

Glassware: Cocktail Glass

Method: Prepare this drink directly in a mixing glass by pouring the ingredients above over ice, stir gently for 20 seconds to allow a generous dilution and to properly chill the cocktail, then strain into a cold cocktail glass.

Garnish: Cherry

STIRRED-UP COCKTAILS

Not to be categorized with sugar-forward shaken cocktails also served in a cocktail glass, this category of drink is most commonly consumed in the evening before or after dinner. These concoctions have character and require the knowledge of how to stir a cocktail.

At their basic level, this category of drink is prepared in a mixing glass and is comprised of a base spirit (such as Gin, or Vodka, or Rum, or Tequila, or Whiskey, or Brandy) which has then been "cranked up a notch" with the addition of a small portion of one or more alcoholic ingredients giving them their "masculine" quality and high alcohol content. Sequentially, the ingredients are stirred in ice, and strained into a previously chilled cocktail glass. The "Manhattan Cocktail" is a prime example; typically comprised of nearly 70% of Rye or Bourbon Whiskey (roughly 2 ¼ fluid ounces when served straight up in a 8 ounce "Cocktail glass"), 28% of Sweet Vermouth (¾ fluid ounces) and 2% of Angostura Bitters.

ACCENT / BITTERS
Bitters, Essential Oils, etc.

ALCOHOLIC MODIFIER
Liqueurs, Cordials, Fortified Wines, etc.

BASE SPIRIT
Gin, Brandy, Vodka, Rum, Tequila, Whisk(e)y, etc.

CHEMISTRY

MANHATTAN CULTURE

The Manhattan is a no-nonsense, gimmick-free cocktail and an iconic classic. Boozy and sophisticated, it embodies the energy and vitality of the city after which it is named. Unlike its Cosmopolitan brother in arms, The Manhattan is more dark, moody, and gentlemanly.

The Manhattan has been prominently referenced in many examples of popular culture and is recognized by cocktail experts as one of the top five drinks of all time. There are plenty of variations and debates over the exact ingredients of this drink, so when ordering, it is best to be very specific as to how it should be made. This drink is a sipper: savor the cinnamon, oak, vanilla, chamomile, dark cherries, and much more. The flavors of this silky cocktail seem to go on forever, which is an impressive quality for a drink that contains only three ingredients.

MANHATTAN HISTORY

As in the case of most classics, the origin of the Manhattan comes in different versions.

It allegedly originated at the Manhattan Club in New York City in the early 1870's when Lady Randolph Churchill, Winston's Churchill's mother, hosted a reception in honor of Presidential Candidate Samuel J. Tilden Peaple. The cocktail created for the occasion was so well received that people requested it referring to it as "The Manhattan Cocktail".

Another story came from William F Mulhall, the bartender at the Hoffman House Hotel between 1862 and 1915. He wrote that the cocktail was invented by a bartender called Black at a bar on Broadway near Houston Street around 1860.

COSMOPOLITAN

Ingredients:
- 1 ½ oz. Citrus Flavored Vodka
- ¾ oz. Premium Orange Liqueur
- ½ oz. Lime Juice
- ½ oz. Cranberry Juice

Glassware: Cocktail Glass

Method: Prepare this drink in a cocktail shaker by pouring the ingredients, adding a scoop of ice and shaking for roughly 10 seconds. Strain into a chilled cocktail glass.

Garnish: Lemon twist

SHAKEN-UP COCKTAILS

Often misnamed "Martinis", and not to be categorized with their all-alcohol cousins also served in a cocktail glass, these concoctions are more fun and fresh and require the knowledge of how to shake and strain a cocktail. At their basic level, this category of drink is comprised of a base spirit (such as Gin, or Vodka, or Rum, or Tequila, or Whiskey, or Brandy) which has then been "flavored" with a small portion of one or more alcoholic ingredients (known as Alcoholic modifiers in this case) in addition to at least one non-alcoholic ingredient (known as Non-Alcoholic mixers in this case) to make them easier to drink and to moderately lower their alcohol content. Sequentially the ingredients are strained into a previously chilled cocktail glass.

The "Cosmopolitan Cocktail" is a prime example; comprised of 50% Citrus Vodka (roughly 1 ½ fluid ounces when served straight up in a 8 ounce "Cocktail glass"), 25% Premium "Triple Sec" Orange Liqueur (¾ fluid ounces) and the remaining 25% non-alcoholic ingredients (Cranberry and Lime juice).

NON-ALCOHOLIC MODIFIER
Sodas, Juices, Creamers, Syrups, etc.

NON-ALCOHOLIC MIXER
Sodas, Juices, Creamers, etc.

ALCOHOLIC MODIFIER
Liqueurs, Cordials, Fortified Wines, etc.

BASE SPIRIT
Gin, Brandy, Vodka, Rum, Tequila, Whisk(e)y, etc.

CHEMISTRY

COSMOPOLITAN CULTURE

The Cosmopolitan (Aka the "Cosmo") is a modern-day classic cocktail and a symbol of sexual and artistic sophistication. While the Cosmo has been around for decades, it was inextricably intertwined into popular culture and gained international admiration in the late 1990's being Carrie Bradshaw's drink of choice on the hit television show Sex and the City.

Most bartenders know how to make this light, fruity, yet tart cocktail, making it a popular choice for a casual night out with friends or colleagues. A recent effort to "manify" the Cosmo through the addition of more cranberry juice has caused this originally light pink cocktail to become redder in color. The best garnish for the Cosmo is open to different interpretations, but the lemon twist, lime wheel and flamed orange peel are common favorites.

COSMOPOLITAN HISTORY

There are several stories related to the creation of this drink, including the idea that John Caine, owner of several bars in San Francisco, developed it in the 1970's.

The most common version credits its origins from South Beach, Florida Bartender Cheryl Cook who came up with the original formula in 1985 using a citrus-flavored vodka that was test marketed in her city.

Two other people who are often credited with having invented the Cosmo are Dale DeGroff, King Cocktail himself, and Toby Cecchini. While both have denied being the creators it is very possible that their improvements on the original recipe enhanced the Cosmopolitan's taste and popularity.

MAI TAI

Ingredients:

- 2 oz. Aged Rum
- ½ oz. Orange Curaçao
- 1 oz. Lime Juice
- ½ oz. Simple Syrup
- ½ oz. Orgeat Syrup

Glassware: Rocks Glass

Method: Prepare this drink in a cocktail shaker by pouring the ingredients above, adding a scoop of ice and shaking for roughly 10 seconds. Strain into a Collins glass over crushed ice (if available).

Garnish: Mint Sprig and optional cherry and pineapple wedge.

ROCKS COCKTAILS

This category is made of cocktails that are typically "shaken" and served in a Collins or Rocks glass. At their basic level, this category of drink is comprised of one or more base spirits (such as Gin, or Vodka, or Rum, or Tequila, or Whiskey, or Brandy) which have then been "flavored" with the addition of a small portion of one or more alcoholic ingredients (known as modifiers in this case) in addition to at least one non-alcoholic ingredient (known as mixers in this case) to make them easier to drink and to moderately lower their alcohol. Consequentially the ingredients are strained into an ice-filled glass.

The classic "Mai Tai" is a prime example of unconventional free-spirited nature of this category of drinks. Far too often modified and simplified; Comprised of 50% Rum(s) (2 fluid ounces when served over ice in a 12 ounce glass), 15% Premium "Orange Curaçao" Orange Liqueur (½ fluid ounces) and the remaining 35% non-alcoholic ingredients (Orgeat syrup, simple syrup and Lime juice).

NON-ALCOHOLIC MODIFIER
Sodas, Juices, Creamers, Syrups, etc.

NON-ALCOHOLIC MIXER
Sodas, Juices, Creamers, etc.

ALCOHOLIC MODIFIER
Liqueurs, Cordials, Fortified Wines, etc.

BASE SPIRIT
Gin, Brandy, Vodka, Rum, Tequila, Whisk(e)y, etc.

ICE
Cube, Cracked, Shaved, etc.

CHEMISTRY

MAI TAI CULTURE

Polynesian Pop Culture (Aka "Tiki") reached its peak of popularity in the mid-20th century. During this period, strong tiki influence could be found in art, architecture, as well as food and beverage, transforming a typical night out into a Luau extravaganza. Rum, pineapples, coconuts, hula skirts, bamboo and tiki totems were all embraced with unbridled enthusiasm.

If you fashion yourself as a Mai Tai drinker, and your ill-mixed concoction comes out red in color, you may have never tried the real deal! This legendary classic has undergone many personality changes, but the classic Mai Tai is simple, refreshing, crisp and packed with flavor.

They're easy to make at home, and fulfill every tropical island poolside cliché, while personifying an era that's on the verge of resurgence.

MAI TAI HISTORY

This Polynesian named drink is 100% American in origin. In 1944 legendary restaurateur Victor Bergeron, created it in Oakland, California at Trader Vic's. As the story goes, he served his newly created concoction to his friends visiting from Tahiti.

One of them took a sip and said, "Mai tai roa ae" (Tahitian to mean "Out of this World"). Victor liked the sound of it and named the drink Mai Tai.

Another story suggests that Don the Beachcomber created a drink called the Mai Tai Swizzle in 1933; however this drink did not stick around for too long and evidence suggests that Trader Vic did not know about Don's creation; furthermore Trader Vic's Mai Tai is the one that became iconic.

MOJITO

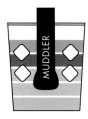

Ingredients:

- 6 - 8 Mint Leaves
- 1 oz. Simple Syrup (equal amounts of sugar and water)
- 1 oz. Fresh Lime Juice
- 2 oz. Light Rum
- Top with Club Soda

Glassware: Collins or Rocks Glass

Method: In a Collins glass, muddle all the fresh mint leaves with the simple sugar and lime juice. Top glass with ice, add the rum and the club soda. Stir well to bring the mint leaves to the top.

Garnish: Mint Sprig

MUDDLED DRINKS

A category of drinks whose principle point of differentiation with all others is the use of a muddler to extract flavors in preparation. These cocktails can be served in different types of glassware.

While Bartenders and Mixologists continue to find different ingredients to muddle from herbs to fruits and spices, it is the actual muddling of these ingredients that make this a stand-alone category.

A prime example of this is seen in a "Mojito", where the combination of fresh mint leaves, lime juice and simple syrup are muddled together to give this cocktail its unique refreshing flavor.

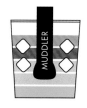

NON-ALCOHOLIC MIXER
Sodas, Juices, Creamers, etc.

SWEETENER
Cane Sugar, Honey, Agave Nectar, etc.

BASE SPIRIT
Gin, Brandy, Vodka, Rum, Tequila, Whisk(e)y, etc.

FRESH FRUIT OR HERB
Fruits, Fresh Berries, Dill, Mint, etc.

ICE
Cube, Cracked, Shaved, etc.

CHEMISTRY

MOJITO CULTURE

The Mojito is as simple and tasty as it looks. This authentic drink requires fresh quality ingredients, attention to detail, and inspiration. The traditional bar *La Bodeguita del Medio*, known by many as the birthplace of the Mojito, is a popular attraction in Havana.

Besides the intriguing culture, you'll have the chance to see legendary signatures on its walls alongside the famous quote, "My mojito in La Bodeguita, My daiquiri in El Floridita", engraved by Ernest Hemingway himself.

Whatever the origins of its heritage, this Cuban cooler has become wildly popular over the last couple of years.

MOJITO HISTORY

Is Cuba the birthplace of the Mojito? Although the exact origin of this classic cocktail is the subject of much debate, many claim it was crafted in Cuba in the late 1800's.

Others elaborate on a theory saying that the mojito was the preferred beverage of Sir Francis Drake as early as the 1500's when the feared privateer tried to sack Havana for its gold.

The story goes that around this same era, a cocktail made with aguardiente (a crude forerunner of rum), sugar, lime and mint was created and named after the famous buccaneer. Cuban playwright and poet Federico Villoch proclaimed, "When aquardiente was replaced with rum, the Draque was to be called a Mojito".

IRISH COFFEE

Ingredients:

- 2 oz. Irish Whiskey
- 4 oz. Hot Coffee
- 1 tsp. Brown Sugar
- 1 oz. Sweetened whipped cream

Glassware: Tempered Glass

Method: Prepare this drink directly in a heat resistant glass by adding the first three ingredients and floating the whipped cream on top.

Garnish: None

This category of drinks includes drinks whose principle point of differentiation from all others is the use of hot ingredients and the importance of skill in pouring ingredients into tempered glassware. At their basic level, this category of drink is "built" directly in the tempered glass and comprises of a base spirit (such as Gin, or Vodka, or Rum, or Tequila, or Whiskey, or Brandy) which has been enhanced and softened with a generous portion of one or more hot ingredients, giving them their characteristically easy-drinking and warming quality.

A prime example of this is seen in an "Irish Coffee"; typically comprised of 50% Brewed Coffee (roughly 4 fluid ounces when served in a 10 ounce mug) and 25% Irish Whiskey (Two fluid ounces), and roughly 25% non-alcoholic ingredients (sugar and whipped Cream).

NON-ALCOHOLIC MIXER
Sodas, Juices, Creamers, etc.

SWEETENER
Cane Sugar, Honey, Agave Nectar, etc.

§§§ HOT INGREDIENT §§§
Coffee, Tea, Chamomile, Hot Water etc.

BASE SPIRIT
Gin, Brandy, Vodka, Rum, Tequila, Whiskey, etc.

CHEMISTRY

IRISH COFFEE CULTURE

The world is obsessed with coffee! Studies have shown that over 50% of Americans would rather gain 10 pounds than give up coffee for life! So, how can this "black mud" get any better? Mixing it with another fast growing American favorite: Irish whiskey! Add some cream and sugar and there you have it: Irish coffee.

Let's face it, few things are as soothing as a warm beverage on a cold, winter day. Whether you're watching football from the stands, or just relaxing at home, the Irish coffee always satisfies. Making this drink requires a bit of skill because layering the cream in the proper way comes with a bit of practice (see page 24 for details).

If the cream doesn't float on top, the presentation will appear sloppy. However, if you have good ingredients it will always taste exquisite regardless of its appearance.

IRISH COFFEE HISTORY

Between 1939 and 1945 many Americans flew to Ireland, and were then shuttled by boat to the terminal. On cold damp days the passengers were somewhat chilled after the ride. They really appreciated a cup of hot coffee or tea upon arrival to the terminal.

The Irish have long taken a little whiskey in their tea. This gave the new chef Joseph Sheridan, an idea. He thought he would treat the newly arrived damp miserable Americans to a little Irish hospitality with an American twist. So in 1942 the Irish coffee recipe was born.

One night in 1952, the owner of the Buena Vista Cafe in San Francisco, Jack Koeppler, and travel writer Stanton Delaplane, decided to recreate the Irish coffee Stanton had tasted while visiting Ireland.

SANGRIA

Ingredients:
- 1 bottle (25.4 oz) Chilled dry red wine
- ½ Cup Brandy
- ¼ Cup Premium Orange Liqueur
- ¼ Cup Orange Juice
- ¼ Cup Simple Syrup
- 2 Cups of mixed cut fruit: Orange, Apple, Lemon and Pear
- 1 Cup cold Club Soda
- 4 Cloves and 2 Cinnamon Sticks

Method: Combine wine, brandy, orange liqueur, orange juice, simple syrup, spices, and fruit in a large glass pitcher.

Cover and chill completely, at least 1 to 2 hours, or overnight. Add soda to mixture when ready to serve. Serve with ice and some of the fruit.

This category of drinks principle point of differentiation from all others is the "marrying" of flavors coming from solid and liquid ingredients for a period of time prior to serving. The important skill of properly timing and trial and error are required.

The trendy barrel-aged cocktails, and more common punch drinks, are a prime example of this family. The most popular drink in this category is a "Sangria", where the combination of fresh fruit, spices, sugar, wine and alcohol take their required time to make a refreshing flavor.

NON-ALCOHOLIC MIXER
Sodas, Juices, Creamers, etc.

NON-ALCOHOLIC MODIFIER
Sodas, Juices, Creamers, Syrups, etc.

ALCOHOLIC MODIFIER
Liqueurs, Cordials, Fortified Wines, etc.

DRIED SPICE
Cloves, Cinnamon, Nutmeg, Allspice, etc.

SWEETENER
Cane Sugar, Honey, Agave Nectar, etc.

FRESH FRUIT OR HERB
Fruits, Fresh Berries, Dill, Mint, etc.

BASE SPIRIT
Gin, Brandy, Vodka, Rum, Tequila, Whisk(e)y, etc.

CHEMISTRY

SANGRIA CULTURE

Sangria is a festive, wine-based, fruity tasting punch cocktail that's a popular choice during the warm summer months. Although it is made with wine, Sangria is perfect for people who aren't real "wine drinkers."

Known for its flavorful combination of premium brandy, wine, fresh fruit, spices and sweeteners, a pitcher of Sangria, coupled with the atmosphere of good company, is what we like to call "perfect sipping." Sangria can range from pleasingly light and refreshing in taste, to "comes with its own health warning", making it popular to accommodate an evening of serious partying. Sangria is ideal for parties or when hosting large groups.

It's fairly difficult to make bad Sangria, but with the right wine and chilling time, great Sangria is the likely result.

SANGRIA HISTORY

The Sangria is the result of Spanish traditions and emerged from the Mediterranean coastal areas where wine and fruit juices have been produced for centuries.

As in the case of most customs and traditions, the history of Sangria unknown but is believed to date back to the Middle Ages.

Since Spain is the Mediterranean country with the richest presence of basic sangria ingredients and where the tradition of mixing wine and fruit juice survived the test of time, the Sangria began to be associated with its Spanish origins.

The name Sangria means "bleeding" and refers to the red color of the wine used as the base in its preparation, similar to the color of blood.

We hope you have enjoyed our book and have found it useful. Our final warning to you is that this book is only as good as the energy you put into following its teachings.

Stay in touch!
We would love to hear your feedback at
info@AummaGroup.com